Table of Contents

Chapter 1: Introduction to the Digital Wild West

In today's interconnected world, social media platforms like Facebook have revolutionized the way we communicate, share information, and connect with others. With over two billion active users worldwide, Facebook has become an integral part of our daily lives, serving as a virtual town square where people gather to socialize, conduct business, and exchange ideas.

However, just as in the Wild West of centuries past, the digital landscape of social media is fraught with dangers and uncertainties. While Facebook offers tremendous opportunities for communication, networking, and entertainment, it also harbors a darker side—a breeding ground for scams, frauds, and malicious activities.

Scammers and cybercriminals operate with anonymity and impunity in this digital Wild West, preying on unsuspecting users with cunning tactics and deceitful schemes. From sophisticated phishing campaigns to elaborate Ponzi schemes, the array of online scams is vast and ever-evolving.

Understanding the landscape of online scams is crucial for safeguarding yourself and your loved ones against potential threats. This introductory chapter serves as a primer on the various types of scams prevalent on Facebook and the importance of vigilance in navigating this digital frontier.

As we embark on this journey to create a safer online community, it's essential to recognize that while Facebook offers countless opportunities for connection and engagement, it also requires us to exercise caution and discernment. By arming ourselves with knowledge and awareness, we can navigate the digital Wild West of social media with confidence and resilience.

Chapter 2: Recognizing Common Scams

Scammers are constantly evolving their tactics to deceive unsuspecting users on Facebook. Understanding the warning signs and common strategies employed by scammers is crucial in protecting yourself from falling victim to their schemes. This chapter delves deeper into some of the most prevalent scams encountered on Facebook:

1. Phishing Links Disguised as Legitimate Websites:

Phishing is a deceptive practice where scammers attempt to trick users into divulging sensitive information, such as login credentials or financial details. They often do this by sending messages or creating posts containing links to fake websites that mimic legitimate ones, such as banking or shopping sites. These phishing links may appear genuine at first glance but are designed to steal your personal information once you input it. It's important to scrutinize URLs carefully and verify the legitimacy of websites before entering any personal data. Here are some phishing scams you might encounter on Facebook:

- Fake Banking Websites:
  -
  You receive a message or see a post on Facebook claiming to be from your bank, alerting you to a security issue with your account.
  -
  The message contains a link to what appears to be your bank's website, asking you to log in to address the supposed security concern.
  -
  However, upon closer inspection, the URL of the website is slightly different from your bank's

official website (e.g., "yourbank-security.com"
instead of "yourbank.com").
-

If you enter your login credentials on this fake
website, the scammer can steal your username
and password, gaining unauthorized access to your
bank account.

- Phony Retail Websites:
  -

  You come across a sponsored post or ad on
  Facebook advertising discounted products from a
  popular retailer.
  -

  The ad includes a link to a website that closely
  resembles the retailer's official site and offers the
  same products at significantly lower prices.
  -

  Excited about the apparent bargain, you click on
  the link and proceed to make a purchase, entering
  your payment information.
  -

  However, the website is a fake replica designed to
  steal your credit card details. Once you enter your
  payment information, the scammer can use it for
  fraudulent purposes.

- False Email Account Login Pages:
  -

  You receive a message or see a post on Facebook
  claiming to be from a popular email service
  provider, stating that your account has been
  compromised.
  -

The message contains a link prompting you to log in to your email account to secure it.
-

The link directs you to a webpage that looks identical to the login page of your email provider, complete with the company's logo and branding.
-

Unbeknownst to you, this page is a phishing site designed to harvest your email login credentials. Once you enter your username and password, the scammer can access your email account and potentially use it for malicious purposes.

It's crucial to remain vigilant and verify the authenticity of websites before entering any sensitive information, especially when prompted to do so via links on social media platforms like Facebook. Always double-check the URL of the website and look for signs of legitimacy, such as HTTPS encryption and official branding, to avoid falling victim to phishing scams. Here are some things to look for when checking the URL to avoid being scammed:

- Domain Name:
  -

  Check the domain name carefully. Scammers often create URLs that resemble legitimate websites but may have slight variations or misspellings. For example, "faceb00k.com" instead of "facebook.com" or "amazon-sale.com" instead of "amazon.com."

  -

  Be wary of domains with uncommon extensions or ones that are not typical for the website you're visiting. For instance, most official websites use

.com, .org, or country-specific extensions like
.co.uk or .gov.

- HTTPS Encryption:
-

Look for HTTPS at the beginning of the URL,
indicating that the website is encrypted and
secure. Legitimate websites, especially those
handling sensitive information like logins or
payments, typically use HTTPS to protect user data.
-

Additionally, reputable browsers often display a
padlock icon next to the URL when the connection
is secure.

- Website Design and Layout:
-

Pay attention to the design and layout of the
website. Legitimate websites often have a
consistent and professional appearance, with high-
quality graphics and clear navigation menus.
-

Be cautious if the website design looks poorly
made, contains spelling or grammatical errors, or
appears significantly different from what you'd
expect from the official site.

- Check for Official Branding:
-

Look for official branding elements such as logos,
colors, and trademarks. Legitimate websites
typically incorporate these elements consistently
throughout their pages.

-

Verify that the branding matches what you would expect from the organization or company associated with the website. If something seems off or inconsistent, it could be a sign of a phishing attempt.

- Hover Over Links:
-

Before clicking on a link, hover your mouse cursor over it to reveal the actual URL. This can help you identify if the link leads to a different website than what is displayed.
-

If the URL shown in the link preview doesn't match the website you expect to visit or looks suspicious, avoid clicking on it.

- Use URL Scanning Tools:
-

Consider using online URL scanning tools or browser extensions that can analyze and verify the legitimacy of URLs. These tools can check for known phishing sites and malware-infected pages before you visit them.

- By being vigilant and examining URLs closely, you can better protect yourself from falling victim to phishing scams and other fraudulent activities on the internet, including those propagated through platforms like Facebook. Remember, when in doubt, it's always safer to refrain from clicking on suspicious links or entering sensitive information.

2. Fake Profiles Impersonating Trusted Individuals or Organizations:

Scammers frequently create fake profiles impersonating trusted individuals, brands, or organizations to gain users' trust and manipulate them into divulging sensitive information or engaging in fraudulent activities. They may use photos and information scraped from legitimate profiles to make their fake accounts appear convincing. Be cautious of friend requests or messages from unfamiliar accounts, especially if they claim to represent someone you know or a reputable entity. Verify the authenticity of the profile through other channels before interacting with them.

Here are some steps you can take to ensure the legitimacy of Facebook profiles and pages:

- Check for Verification Badges:
  -
  Facebook provides verification badges for certain profiles and pages to indicate their authenticity and official status. Look for a blue checkmark badge next to the profile or page name, which signifies that Facebook has confirmed the account's authenticity.
  -
  Keep in mind that not all legitimate profiles or pages may have verification badges, especially smaller businesses, or personal accounts. However, the presence of a verification badge adds an extra layer of credibility.
- Review Profile Information:
  -

Examine the profile or page information carefully for completeness and accuracy. Legitimate profiles and pages typically include detailed information about the individual or organization, such as a bio, contact information, website links, and background details.

-

Pay attention to inconsistencies or discrepancies in the profile information, such as misspellings, incorrect contact details, or vague descriptions. Scammers may overlook these details when creating fake profiles or pages.

- Analyze Content and Activity:

-

Review the content posted on the profile or page, including status updates, photos, videos, and links. Legitimate profiles and pages often share relevant and engaging content related to their interests, industry, or mission.

-

Look for signs of engagement and interaction, such as likes, comments, and shares from genuine users. A lack of engagement or suspicious activity, such as repetitive posts or spammy comments, could indicate a fake profile or page.

- Verify External Links and References:

-

If the profile or page links to an external website or references other online sources, verify the legitimacy of these links independently. Visit the linked websites directly to confirm their authenticity and ensure they align with the information provided on the Facebook profile or page.

-

Be cautious of profiles or pages that redirect you to unfamiliar or suspicious websites, especially if they request sensitive information or payment.

- Cross-Check Information:

  -

  Cross-reference information provided on the profile or page with other sources to confirm its accuracy and legitimacy. Search for the individual or organization's name on reputable search engines or review their presence on other social media platforms.

  -

  Look for official websites, press releases, or news articles that corroborate the details provided on the Facebook profile or page. Legitimate entities often have a consistent online presence across multiple platforms.

- Contact Directly or Seek Confirmation:

  -

  If you're still unsure about the authenticity of a Facebook profile or page, consider reaching out directly to the individual or organization through other channels, such as email or phone.

  -

  Alternatively, you can contact Facebook's support team to report suspicious profiles or pages and request verification or clarification on their authenticity.

By following these steps and exercising caution when interacting with Facebook profiles and pages, you can reduce the risk of falling victim to scams and fraudulent activities. Remember to trust your instincts and err on the side of caution if something seems off or too good to be true.

3. Bogus Investment Opportunities Promising Unrealistic Returns:

Investment scams proliferate on social media platforms like Facebook, enticing users with promises of high returns on their investments. These scams often involve fraudulent schemes such as cryptocurrency investments, pyramid schemes, or fake stock offerings. Scammers may use persuasive language and testimonials to lure victims into investing their money, only to disappear with the funds once they've been transferred. Exercise caution when approached with investment opportunities on Facebook and conduct thorough research before committing any funds.

Here are some examples of bogus investment opportunities promising unrealistic returns that one might encounter on Facebook:

- Cryptocurrency Ponzi Schemes:
  - You come across a Facebook ad or post promoting a new cryptocurrency investment opportunity promising guaranteed high returns within a short period.
  - The investment scheme requires you to recruit new investors and promises even greater returns through referral bonuses.
  - The scheme claims to use sophisticated trading algorithms or strategies to generate profits but lacks transparency about its operations or the risks involved.
  - However, upon closer inspection, the scheme resembles a classic Ponzi scheme, where returns for earlier investors are paid using funds from new investors, rather than through legitimate investments.

- Forex Trading Scams:
  - You receive a friend request or message from a Facebook user claiming to be a successful forex trader offering to teach you their trading strategies for a fee.
  - The trader boasts of consistently high returns and promises to help you achieve similar profits by following their advice or joining their trading group.
  - They may even provide screenshots of supposed profits or testimonials from satisfied clients to lend credibility to their claims.
  - However, upon further investigation, you discover that the trader lacks credentials or a verifiable track record, and their strategies are not based on sound financial principles.
- Fake Investment Funds or Programs:
  - You encounter a sponsored post or ad on Facebook promoting an investment fund or program promising extraordinarily high returns with minimal risk.
  - The investment opportunity may claim to invest in lucrative markets such as real estate, commodities, or startups, offering returns far above market averages.
  - The promoters may use persuasive language and testimonials to entice potential investors, emphasizing the urgency of taking advantage of the opportunity before it's too late.

-

However, upon scrutiny, you find that the investment fund lacks regulatory oversight or credible documentation, and the promised returns are unrealistic or unsustainable.

- Pyramid or Multi-Level Marketing (MLM) Schemes:
  -

  You receive an invitation to join a Facebook group or event promoting a business opportunity that promises to make you rich by selling products or recruiting others to join the scheme.
  -

  The scheme requires an upfront investment or purchase of inventory, with the promise of earning commissions from sales made by your recruits or downline.
  -

  The promoters exaggerate the income potential and downplay the risks associated with participating in the scheme, emphasizing the lifestyle benefits of becoming a successful entrepreneur.
  -

  However, the scheme operates on a pyramid structure, where profits primarily come from recruitment rather than the sale of legitimate products or services, making it unsustainable in the long run.
- It's important to approach any investment opportunity on Facebook with caution and skepticism, especially if it promises unrealistically high returns with minimal risk. Conduct thorough research, seek advice from financial professionals, and be wary of schemes that sound too good to be

true. Remember, legitimate investments involve calculated risks and realistic expectations, not get-rich-quick schemes.

4. Sweepstakes or Giveaways Requiring Personal Information or Payment:

Fake sweepstakes or giveaways are a common tactic used by scammers to collect personal information or extort money from unsuspecting users. They may create posts or ads claiming that users have won prizes such as gift cards, vacations, or electronic gadgets, but require them to provide personal information or pay a fee to claim their winnings. Legitimate sweepstakes do not require payment or sensitive information upfront, so be wary of any requests for such details. Verify the authenticity of the giveaway by researching the sponsoring company or contacting them directly.

Here are some examples of sweepstakes or giveaways requiring personal information or payment that one might encounter on Facebook:

- **Fake Prize Giveaways:**
  - You come across a post or sponsored ad on Facebook claiming to offer the chance to win a high-value prize, such as a luxury vacation, electronic gadgets, or gift cards.
  - The giveaway requires participants to like, share, and comment on the post to enter, often with the condition of also providing personal information such as email addresses or phone numbers.
  - Additionally, the giveaway may request payment of a small fee or shipping charges to claim the

prize, under the guise of covering expenses or
processing fees.
-

However, upon closer inspection, you realize that
the giveaway is a scam designed to collect personal
information or money from unsuspecting
participants, with no intention of awarding the
promised prizes.

- Phony Contests or Surveys:
    -

    You receive a message or notification on Facebook
    inviting you to participate in a contest or survey
    promising the chance to win valuable prizes or
    cash rewards.
    -

    The contest or survey requires you to click on a link
    provided in the message and complete a series of
    questions or tasks, which may include sharing
    personal information, downloading apps, or
    signing up for services.
    -

    The scammers behind the contest or survey may
    use deceptive tactics to trick participants into
    providing sensitive information, such as pretending
    to represent well-known brands or organizations.
    -

    However, once you've completed the survey or
    tasks, you discover that there are no prizes to be
    won, and your personal information may be used
    for nefarious purposes such as identity theft or
    phishing attacks.

- Bogus Fundraising Campaigns:

-

You encounter a post or ad on Facebook soliciting donations for a purported charitable cause or emergency relief fund, claiming to help individuals or communities in need.

-

The fundraising campaign may tug at your heartstrings with emotional appeals and heartwarming stories, urging you to contribute money or supplies to support the cause.

-

However, upon closer scrutiny, you realize that the fundraising campaign lacks transparency or legitimacy, with no clear information about how donations will be used or who is organizing the effort.

-

Scammers may exploit the goodwill of generous donors by pocketing the funds themselves or using them for personal gain, rather than assisting those in genuine need.

- Prize Claim Scams:

-

You receive a message or notification on Facebook informing you that you've won a prize in a contest or giveaway, despite not having entered any such competition.

-

The message instructs you to provide personal information or payment details to claim the prize, such as your name, address, phone number, or credit card information.

-

However, this is a scam designed to trick you into divulging sensitive information or making payments to fraudsters, with no legitimate prize awaiting you at the end.

It's important to exercise caution when encountering sweepstakes or giveaways on Facebook, especially if they require you to provide personal information or payment details. Legitimate giveaways typically do not require payment to enter, and they do not ask for sensitive information such as credit card numbers or social security numbers. Be wary of any requests for personal information or payments and verify the legitimacy of the giveaway before participating.

By familiarizing yourself with these common scams and remaining vigilant while browsing Facebook, you can significantly reduce your risk of falling victim to fraudulent activities. Remember to always verify the legitimacy of offers or requests before sharing personal information or engaging in financial transactions online. In the digital age, knowledge and awareness are your best defenses against scams on Facebook.

Chapter 3: Guarding Your Personal Information

Your personal information is invaluable, serving as the cornerstone of your identity both online and offline. Scammers and cybercriminals are constantly on the lookout for opportunities to exploit this information for their nefarious purposes, making it essential to safeguard your data at all costs. This chapter delves into practical strategies for protecting your privacy on Facebook and minimizing the risk of falling victim to identity theft or other forms of fraud.

1. Adjusting Privacy Settings:

  - Facebook offers a range of privacy settings that allow you to control who can see your posts, photos, and personal information. Take the time to review and adjust these settings to ensure they align with your preferences and comfort level.

  - Consider setting your profile to private or limiting the visibility of your posts to friends only. You can also customize privacy settings for individual posts to restrict access to specific groups or individuals.

  - Regularly review and update your privacy settings as Facebook's features and options may change over time. Stay informed about new privacy controls and adjust them accordingly to maintain control over your personal information.

Here's a more detailed breakdown of how to adjust these settings effectively:

- Accessing Privacy Settings:
  -

To access your privacy settings on Facebook, click on the downward-facing arrow in the top right corner of the Facebook homepage and select "Settings & Privacy" from the dropdown menu.

-

From the expanded menu, click on "Privacy Checkup" or "Privacy Shortcuts" to access various privacy settings.

- Facebook regularly updates its layout so these exact items may be located elsewhere. If following these exact instructions doesn't get you there, look for a general settings page and then scan for the keywords listed above to get to the right place.

- Setting Profile Privacy:

-

Navigate to the "Privacy Shortcuts" section and click on "Privacy Checkup."

-

Review the options under "Your Activity" to adjust who can see your future posts, who can send you friend requests, and who can see your friends list.

-

Consider setting your future posts to "Friends" or a custom list to limit visibility to only those you trust.

-

Under "How People Find You on Facebook," you can control who can send you friend requests, search for you using your email address or phone number and see your friend requests.

-

Set these options according to your preferences, such as restricting friend requests to friends of friends or limiting search visibility to friends only.

- Customizing Post Privacy:

- When creating a new post or sharing content on Facebook, you can customize the privacy settings for that specific post.
- Click on the privacy dropdown menu located below your name and profile picture before posting.
- Choose from options such as "Public," "Friends," "Friends except," or "Specific friends" to control who can see the post.
- You can also customize visibility for specific groups or individuals by selecting "More options" and entering their names.

- Reviewing Tagging and Timeline Visibility:
  - Navigate to the "Timeline and Tagging" section in your privacy settings to review who can post on your timeline, who can see posts you've been tagged in, and who can see posts on your timeline.
  - Adjust these settings to control who can tag you in posts and who can see posts that others tag you in.

- Updating Privacy Settings Regularly:
  - Facebook's features and privacy options may change over time, so it's essential to review and update your privacy settings regularly.
  - Stay informed about new privacy controls and features by checking Facebook's Help Center or following official Facebook announcements.
  -

Periodically review your privacy settings to ensure they align with your current preferences and comfort level.
- By taking the time to review and adjust your privacy settings on Facebook, you can maintain control over your personal information and posts, limiting access to only those you trust. Regularly updating these settings ensures that you stay informed about changes and can adapt your privacy preferences accordingly.

2. Being Cautious About Sharing Sensitive Details:

- Exercise caution when sharing sensitive information such as your address, phone number, or financial details on Facebook. Avoid posting this information publicly or in response to unsolicited messages or requests.

- Be mindful of what you share in your Facebook profile and posts, as even seemingly innocuous details can be exploited by scammers to piece together your identity or perpetrate fraud.

- Think twice before sharing personal information in comments, chat messages, or on public forums, as these interactions may not be as private as you think.

Here are some specific examples of posts that individuals might encounter or be tempted to share on Facebook, which could inadvertently result in sharing sensitive personal details and potentially open them up to being scammed:

- Vacation Updates:
  -
  Example: "Having an amazing time on vacation in Hawaii! ☐ So grateful for this getaway!"
  -

Potential Risk: Sharing real-time updates about your vacation can alert potential scammers that your home is vacant, making it a target for burglary. Additionally, publicly disclosing your travel plans may expose you to targeted phishing attempts or scams posing as travel-related services.

When posting about vacation updates on Facebook, it's essential to balance sharing your experiences with protecting your privacy and security. Here are some alternative, safer options for sharing vacation updates:

- o Post After Returning:
    - o Instead of sharing real-time updates while on vacation, wait until you've returned home before posting about your trip. This way, you won't inadvertently alert potential burglars that your home is vacant.

- o Share Highlights:
    - o Instead of providing detailed updates about your exact location and itinerary, share general highlights or photos from your trip after returning. Focus on the positive aspects of your vacation experience without revealing specific dates or locations.

- o Use Privacy Settings:
    - o Utilize Facebook's privacy settings to control who can see your vacation posts. Consider limiting the visibility of your vacation updates to a select group

of close friends or family members
rather than making them public.

- o Share Memories:
    - o Instead of sharing updates in real-time,
      consider sharing memories or
      reflections about your vacation after
      returning. Share anecdotes, photos, or
      videos that highlight the enjoyable
      moments of your trip without
      compromising your privacy.

- o Avoid Mentioning Length of Absence:
    - o Refrain from mentioning the duration
      of your absence in your vacation posts.
      Avoid phrases like "gone for two weeks"
      or "back in a month," as this
      information can be useful to potential
      burglars.

- o Notify Trusted Contacts Privately:
    - o If necessary, notify trusted friends or
      neighbors privately about your vacation
      plans, especially if you'll be away for an
      extended period. This way, they can
      keep an eye on your property and help
      ensure your home's security while
      you're away.

- o By adopting these safer options for sharing
  vacation updates on Facebook, you can enjoy
  sharing your travel experiences while
  minimizing the risk of becoming a target for

burglaries or scams. Remember to prioritize your privacy and security when posting on social media platforms.

- Personal Milestones:
    - Example: "Excited to announce that I just bought my first home! □ #NewHomeowner"
    - Potential Risk: Celebrating personal milestones such as buying a new home or car may inadvertently disclose sensitive information such as your address or financial status. Scammers could use this information to target you with fraudulent schemes or identity theft.

When posting about personal milestones on Facebook, it's important to strike a balance between sharing your achievements and protecting your privacy and security. Here are some alternative, safer options for sharing personal milestones:

    - Share Without Specific Details:
        - Instead of providing specific details such as buying a new home or car, share the excitement of your milestone without disclosing sensitive information. For example, you could post, "Feeling grateful for reaching a significant milestone in my life! □ #PersonalGrowth"

    - Focus on General Achievements:
        - Share the broader accomplishment or milestone without mentioning specific

purchases or acquisitions. For instance, you could post, "Celebrating a major achievement today! Grateful for the journey and looking forward to what's next! □ #MilestoneReached"

- o Avoid Mentioning Financial Details:
    - o Refrain from mentioning financial details or specifics about the purchase, such as the cost of the home or car. Avoid phrases like "Just closed on my dream home!" or "Bought a luxury car today!" to prevent inadvertently disclosing sensitive information.

- o Share Privately or in a Closed Group:
    - o Consider sharing personal milestones in private messages or within closed Facebook groups consisting of close friends and family members. This limits the visibility of your post to a select audience, reducing the risk of exposing sensitive information to potential scammers.

- o Celebrate Without Location Details:
    - o Avoid mentioning specific location details or addresses in your post. Instead, focus on the emotional significance of the milestone and how it makes you feel. For example, "Thrilled to achieve a significant milestone in my life! Grateful for the support of my

loved ones along the way. ♥ ☐
#PersonalGrowth"

- o Share Offline:
    - o Alternatively, celebrate your personal milestones offline with close friends and family members rather than broadcasting them on social media platforms. You can share the news privately and in person, maintaining a greater level of privacy and security.

By adopting these safer options for posting about personal milestones on Facebook, you can still celebrate your achievements while safeguarding your privacy and security. Remember to be mindful of the information you share online and consider the potential risks before making personal details public.

- • Financial Successes:
    - o Example: "Just landed my dream job with a six-figure salary! ☐ #Blessed"
    - o Potential Risk: Sharing details about significant financial achievements or windfalls can make you a target for investment scams or fraudulent schemes promising to help you manage or invest your newfound wealth. Scammers may exploit your perceived financial success to lure you into risky or illegitimate ventures.

When sharing about financial successes on Facebook, it's crucial to exercise caution and avoid inadvertently attracting scammers. Here are alternative, safer options for sharing financial achievements:

- o Share Generically:
  - o Instead of providing specific details about your financial success, share the excitement of reaching a career milestone in a more generic way. For example, you could post, "Feeling grateful for new opportunities and growth in my career! □ #ProfessionalAchievement"

- o Focus on Career Growth:
  - o Highlight the professional aspects of your achievement without disclosing specific salary figures or financial details. Share your excitement about career advancements or new opportunities without mentioning monetary gains.

- o Celebrate Privately:
  - o Consider celebrating your financial successes privately with close friends, family members, or trusted individuals rather than broadcasting them on social media. This reduces the risk of attracting unwanted attention from scammers.

- o Avoid Mentioning Specific Salary Figures:
  - o Refrain from mentioning specific salary figures or exact financial details in your post. Instead, focus on the personal satisfaction and fulfillment derived from achieving career goals. For example,

"Thrilled to have reached a significant milestone in my career journey! Grateful for the support of my mentors and colleagues. ☐ #CareerGrowth"

- o Share without Hashtags:
  - o Avoid using hashtags that may draw unnecessary attention to your post, such as "#Blessed" or "#SixFigureSalary." While these hashtags may seem innocent, they can inadvertently attract scammers or individuals looking to exploit your success.

- o Maintain Discretion:
  - o Exercise discretion when sharing about financial successes on social media platforms. Consider the potential risks and implications of making such information public before posting. When in doubt, err on the side of caution and refrain from sharing specific financial details online.

By adopting these safer options for sharing about financial successes on Facebook, you can celebrate your achievements without exposing yourself to potential scams or fraudulent schemes. Remember to prioritize your privacy and security when posting on social media platforms, especially when it comes to sensitive financial information.

- • Personal Identification Documents:

- o   Example: "Finally got my driver's license renewed! Here's a photo of it! □ #OfficiallyLegal"
- o   Potential Risk: Sharing images or details of personal identification documents such as driver's licenses, passports, or social security cards exposes you to identity theft and fraud. Scammers could use this information to impersonate you or commit identity fraud, potentially causing significant financial and reputational harm.

When it comes to personal identification documents, it's crucial to refrain from sharing images or details on social media platforms like Facebook. Here are alternative, safer options for sharing updates without compromising your personal security:

- o   Share the Update Without the Document:
    - o   Instead of posting a photo or details of your personal identification document, simply share the update without including the document. For example, you could post, "Finally got my driver's license renewed! Feels good to be legal again! □ #RoadReady"

- o   Celebrate Without Revealing Specifics:
    - o   Focus on the milestone itself rather than sharing specific details about the document. Avoid mentioning the type of document or providing identifying information. For instance, you could post, "Celebrating an important renewal milestone today! Grateful for

smooth processes and efficient services.
□ #MilestoneReached"

- o Use General Terms:
  - o Refrain from using terms or hashtags that imply sharing personal identification information. Avoid phrases like "officially legal" or "ID renewal" in your post or hashtags to minimize the risk of drawing attention to sensitive documents.

- o Share Offline:
  - o Celebrate personal milestones like document renewals offline with friends and family members rather than sharing them on social media. You can share the news privately and in person, maintaining a greater level of privacy and security.

- o Educate Others:
  - o Instead of sharing personal identification documents, consider posting about the importance of safeguarding personal information and the risks associated with sharing sensitive documents online. Raise awareness about identity theft and fraud without revealing your own personal details.

- o Remove or Report Any Posts with Personal Documents:
    - o If you come across posts from others sharing personal identification documents, refrain from engaging with them and consider reporting the content to Facebook. Help protect others' privacy by not sharing or endorsing such posts.

  - o By refraining from sharing images or details of personal identification documents on Facebook and opting for safer alternatives, you can protect yourself from identity theft and fraud. Remember to prioritize your privacy and security when posting on social media platforms, especially when it comes to sensitive personal information.

- Survey or Quiz Participation:
    - o Example: "Just completed this fun quiz to find out which Disney character I am! Check it out and let me know your results! □"
    - o Potential Risk: Participating in surveys or quizzes on Facebook may require granting access to personal information such as your profile data, friends list, or email address. Scammers could use this information for targeted phishing attacks, spam, or identity theft, posing as legitimate businesses or organizations.

When it comes to participating in surveys or quizzes on Facebook, it's important to prioritize your privacy and security. Here are alternative, safer options for engaging in similar activities without risking exposure to scams or identity theft:

- o Use Third-Party Quiz Platforms:
  - o Instead of participating in quizzes directly on Facebook, consider using reputable third-party quiz platforms or websites that prioritize user privacy and security. Look for platforms with clear privacy policies and a good reputation for protecting user data.

- o Research the Quiz Provider:
  - o Before participating in a quiz, research the provider or organization offering the quiz to ensure their legitimacy and credibility. Look for reviews or feedback from other users to gauge their trustworthiness.

- o Review Privacy Settings:
  - o Review and adjust your Facebook privacy settings to limit the information that third-party apps and quizzes can access. Consider restricting access to only necessary information and avoiding granting permissions for sensitive data.

- o Avoid Personal Questions:
  - o Be cautious when participating in quizzes that ask for personal information beyond what is necessary

for the quiz's purpose. Refrain from answering questions that seem overly intrusive or unrelated to the quiz topic.

- o Read Terms and Conditions:
    - o Before participating in a quiz, carefully read the terms and conditions, as well as the privacy policy, to understand how your data will be used and shared. Avoid quizzes that have vague or ambiguous terms regarding data usage.

- o Create Dummy Accounts:
    - o Consider using a dummy or secondary Facebook account specifically for participating in quizzes or surveys. Use this account to limit the exposure of your personal information while still engaging in these activities.

- o Be Selective:
    - o Be selective about the quizzes you choose to participate in and avoid clicking on random quiz links shared by unfamiliar sources. Stick to quizzes from reputable providers and organizations to minimize the risk of exposure to scams or phishing attempts.

- o By following these alternative, safer options for participating in quizzes or surveys on Facebook, you can enjoy similar activities without compromising your privacy or security.

Remember to always prioritize caution and discretion when sharing personal information online.

- Clickbait or Phishing Links:
    - Example: "Click here to claim your free iPhone X! Limited time offer! □"
    - Potential Risk: Clicking on links shared in enticing posts or ads promising freebies, discounts, or exclusive offers could lead to phishing scams, malware downloads, or identity theft. Scammers use clickbait tactics to lure users into clicking on malicious links that compromise their personal information or device security.

Identifying clickbait versus legitimate offers on Facebook requires a combination of critical thinking, skepticism, and familiarity with common tactics used by scammers and legitimate advertisers. Here are some key details to help you differentiate between the two:

- Sensational Headlines:
    - Clickbait: Clickbait posts often use sensational or exaggerated headlines designed to grab attention and evoke curiosity. They may make bold claims or promises to lure users into clicking on the link.
    - Legitimate Offers: Legitimate offers typically use clear and concise headlines that accurately describe the product or service being offered. They avoid using exaggerated language or making unrealistic promises.

- o Misleading Images or Thumbnails:
    - o Clickbait: Clickbait posts often use misleading images or thumbnails that are unrelated to the content being promoted. They may use sensational or provocative images to entice users to click.
    - o Legitimate Offers: Legitimate offers use relevant and appropriate images or thumbnails that accurately represent the product or service being advertised. They avoid using deceptive imagery to attract clicks.

- o Unrealistic Claims or Promises:
    - o Clickbait: Clickbait posts frequently make unrealistic claims or promises, such as "Get rich quick" schemes or "Lose 10 pounds in one week" diets. They may use hyperbolic language to exaggerate the benefits of clicking on the link.
    - o Legitimate Offers: Legitimate offers provide realistic and achievable benefits or solutions. They avoid making extravagant claims or promises that seem too good to be true.

- o Lack of Credible Sources or References:
    - o Clickbait: Clickbait posts often lack credible sources or references to support their claims. They may rely on anecdotal evidence or vague

testimonials to give the appearance of legitimacy.
  - Legitimate Offers: Legitimate offers provide credible sources or references to back up their claims. They may include customer reviews, endorsements from reputable sources, or scientific studies to support the effectiveness of their product or service.

- Hidden or Obfuscated Information:
  - Clickbait: Clickbait posts may hide or obfuscate important information, such as the true nature of the offer or the terms and conditions associated with it. They may use deceptive tactics to trick users into clicking without fully understanding what they're getting into.
  - Legitimate Offers: Legitimate offers provide transparent and upfront information about the product or service being offered, including pricing, terms of use, and any limitations or restrictions. They avoid hiding or obfuscating important details that could mislead users.

- Trustworthiness of the Source:
  - Clickbait: Clickbait posts often come from unreliable or questionable sources, such as unknown websites or unverified social media accounts. They may lack credibility and transparency,

       making it difficult to verify the legitimacy of the offer.

- o Legitimate Offers: Legitimate offers typically come from reputable and established brands, businesses, or organizations with a track record of reliability and trustworthiness. They may have a verified presence on Facebook and a strong reputation among customers or users.

- o By considering these key details and exercising caution when encountering posts on Facebook, you can better distinguish between clickbait and legitimate offers. Remember to verify the credibility of the source, critically evaluate the claims being made, and avoid clicking on posts that seem suspicious or too good to be true.

It's essential to exercise caution and think critically before sharing personal details or engaging with posts on Facebook. Avoid oversharing sensitive information and be skeptical of offers or requests that seem too good to be true. By being mindful of the information you share online, you can reduce the risk of falling victim to scams and protect your privacy and security.

3. Avoiding Third-Party Apps and Quizzes:

  - Be wary of third-party apps, games, or quizzes on Facebook that request access to your profile data. These apps may harvest your personal information, including your friends list, likes, and preferences, for advertising or other purposes.

  - Before granting access to a third-party app or participating in a quiz, carefully review the permissions requested and consider whether they are necessary for the app's functionality. Avoid granting access to sensitive information unless absolutely necessary.

   - Regularly review the list of apps connected to your Facebook account and remove any that you no longer use or trust. Limiting the number of apps with access to your data can help reduce the risk of unauthorized access or misuse.

Avoiding third-party apps and quizzes on Facebook is crucial for protecting your privacy and data security. Here's more detail on how to do so effectively:

- **Understanding Permissions:**
    - When you encounter a third-party app or quiz on Facebook, carefully review the permissions it requests before granting access. These permissions may include accessing your profile information, friends list, email address, and other personal data.
    - Consider whether the requested permissions are necessary for the app's functionality. Be skeptical of apps that ask for access to more information than is required for their stated purpose, as this could be a red flag for potential misuse of your data.

- **Limiting Access to Sensitive Information:**
    - Avoid granting access to sensitive information unless absolutely necessary. Be cautious about apps or quizzes that request access to your personal messages, location data, or other sensitive details.

- o If an app or quiz asks for access to sensitive information, consider whether you trust the provider and whether the benefits of using the app outweigh the risks of sharing your data.

- **Reviewing App Permissions:**
  - o Regularly review the list of apps connected to your Facebook account to monitor the access they have to your data. You can do this by accessing your Facebook settings and navigating to the "Apps and Websites" section.
  - o Remove any apps that you no longer use or trust by clicking on the app's name and selecting "Remove App." This helps reduce the risk of unauthorized access or misuse of your personal information.

- **Being Selective with App Installation:**
  - o Exercise caution when installing new apps or participating in quizzes on Facebook. Stick to apps and quizzes from reputable sources, such as well-known brands, businesses, or developers with a proven track record of respecting user privacy.
  - o Avoid clicking on suspicious links or ads that lead to third-party apps or quizzes, especially if they seem too good to be true or request excessive permissions.

- **Using App Privacy Controls:**
  - o Take advantage of Facebook's privacy controls for apps to manage the

information you share with third-party apps. You can adjust these settings by accessing your Facebook settings and navigating to the "Apps and Websites" section.

- o Review and edit the information that apps can access, such as your public profile, friends list, and email address, to limit the data shared with third-party providers.

- By following these guidelines and being vigilant about the apps and quizzes you interact with on Facebook, you can minimize the risk of unauthorized access to your personal information and protect your privacy and data security. Remember to prioritize caution and discretion when granting access to third-party apps and only share sensitive information with trusted sources.

By implementing these practical tips for guarding your personal information on Facebook, you can minimize the risk of falling victim to identity theft, phishing scams, and other forms of online fraud. Remember, your privacy is paramount, and taking proactive steps to protect it is essential in today's digital age. Stay vigilant, stay informed, and stay safe online.

Chapter 4: Verifying Authenticity

In the vast expanse of social media, distinguishing between genuine and counterfeit accounts or content can be akin to navigating through murky waters. However, mastering the art of verifying authenticity is paramount in safeguarding oneself from scams and fraudulent activities. This chapter delves into comprehensive guidance on how to discern the real from the fake:

1. Verification Badges:

  - Many social media platforms, including Facebook, employ verification badges to authenticate the identity of official accounts. Look for blue checkmarks or similar badges next to the account name, indicating that the profile has been verified as authentic by the platform.

  - Keep in mind that while verification badges lend credibility to an account, they are not foolproof. Scammers may attempt to impersonate verified accounts or create convincing counterfeit badges. Therefore, it's crucial to complement badge verification with other authenticity checks.

2. Content Scrutiny:

  - Scrutinize the content shared by accounts for inconsistencies or red flags. Look for spelling or grammatical errors, unusual posting patterns, or discrepancies in information provided. Authentic accounts typically maintain a consistent tone, style, and quality in their content.

  - Be wary of accounts that excessively promote products or services, engage in sensationalism, or spread misinformation.

Legitimate accounts focus on providing valuable and informative content rather than resorting to clickbait tactics or deceptive practices.

3. Cross-Referencing Information:

 - Verify the information provided by accounts on Facebook by cross-referencing it with trusted sources outside the platform. Consult official websites, reputable news outlets, or credible organizations to validate claims, announcements, or news shared by accounts.

 - Pay attention to whether the information aligns with established facts or corroborates with multiple reliable sources. Exercise caution when encountering content that lacks substantiation or contradicts widely accepted knowledge.

4. Engagement Analysis:

 - Analyze the engagement metrics of accounts, such as the number of followers, likes, comments, and shares. While a high engagement rate can indicate popularity, it can also be artificially inflated through the purchase of followers or engagement bots.

 - Look for meaningful interactions and genuine engagement from users rather than superficial metrics. Authentic accounts foster genuine connections with their audience through meaningful dialogue and interaction.

5. Profile Verification Tools:

 - Utilize profile verification tools or services offered by third-party platforms to assess the authenticity of accounts on Facebook. These tools analyze various factors, including account activity, follower demographics, and engagement patterns, to determine the likelihood of an account being genuine.

- Exercise caution when using third-party verification tools and ensure that they are reputable and trustworthy. Beware of scams or fraudulent services that claim to verify accounts but may compromise your privacy or security.

By employing a multi-faceted approach to verifying authenticity on Facebook, you can navigate the digital landscape with confidence and minimize the risk of falling victim to scams or deceptive practices. Remember to remain vigilant, question suspicious accounts or content, and seek validation from reliable sources before trusting information encountered on social media.

Chapter 5: Exercising Caution in Communication

In the vast digital realm of Facebook, interacting with strangers or unfamiliar entities poses significant risks. From private messages to comments and friend requests, exercising caution in your communication is paramount to safeguarding yourself against scams and fraudulent activities. This chapter delves into comprehensive strategies for staying safe while navigating interactions on the platform:

1. Avoiding Suspicious Links and Attachments:

   - Resist the temptation to click on suspicious links or download attachments from unknown senders, as they may contain malware, phishing attempts, or other harmful content. Exercise vigilance when encountering unsolicited messages or posts that prompt you to click on links or download files.

2. Verifying Identity Before Sharing Personal Information:

   - Before sharing personal information with individuals on Facebook, take steps to verify their identity and legitimacy. Scrutinize their profile for signs of authenticity, such as profile completeness, activity history, and connections.

   - Be cautious when engaging in conversations that request sensitive information, such as your address, phone number, or financial details. Avoid disclosing personal information unless you have verified the identity and trustworthiness of the individual.

3. Exercising Caution in Financial Transactions:

- Exercise extreme caution when engaging in financial transactions with individuals or entities on Facebook. Be skeptical of offers that seem too good to be true or involve sending money to unfamiliar individuals.

- Verify the credibility and legitimacy of individuals or businesses offering goods or services before proceeding with financial transactions. Look for reviews, ratings, or testimonials from other users, and consider using secure payment methods that offer buyer protection.

4. Reporting and Blocking Suspicious Accounts:

- Act promptly to report and block suspicious accounts to prevent further contact and protect yourself and others from potential harm. Facebook provides tools for reporting suspicious behavior, fake accounts, or abusive content.

- Utilize the "Report" and "Block" features to flag suspicious accounts or messages and prevent them from contacting you again. By reporting suspicious activity, you contribute to maintaining a safer online environment for all users.

5. Exercising Discretion in Friend Requests:

- Be discerning when accepting friend requests from individuals you don't know personally. Consider whether the requester has mutual connections, a complete profile, and genuine interactions before accepting the request.

- Avoid accepting friend requests from suspicious or unfamiliar accounts, especially those with limited profile information or suspicious activity. Exercise caution when sharing personal updates or information with your Facebook friends to maintain privacy and security.

By adhering to these comprehensive strategies for exercising caution in communication on Facebook, you can minimize the risk of falling victim to scams, phishing attempts, or fraudulent activities. Remember to remain vigilant, trust your instincts, and prioritize your safety and security while engaging with others on the platform.

Chapter 6: Educating Yourself and Others

In the ever-evolving landscape of social media, knowledge stands as your most formidable defense against scams on Facebook. By arming yourself with awareness and disseminating insights to others, you contribute to fostering a safer online community for all. This final chapter delves into the critical importance of ongoing education and awareness, offering guidance on how to stay informed and protect yourself and others from falling victim to scams:

1. Staying Informed About Scam Trends and Tactics:

   - Stay abreast of the latest scam trends and tactics employed by fraudsters on Facebook. Regularly seek out reliable sources of information, such as reputable news outlets, cybersecurity blogs, or official announcements from Facebook.

   - Familiarize yourself with common scam techniques, such as phishing, identity theft, pyramid schemes, and fake giveaways. Be vigilant for new variations or iterations of these scams and adapt your defenses accordingly.

2. Educating Friends and Family About Common Scams:

   - Share your knowledge and insights about common scams with friends and family members to empower them to recognize and avoid potential threats. Educate them about red flags to watch out for, such as unsolicited requests for personal information, suspicious links, or unrealistic offers.

- Encourage open dialogue and discussion about online safety and security within your social circles. Foster a culture of mutual support and collaboration, where individuals feel comfortable seeking advice and guidance from one another.

3. Reporting Fraudulent Activity to Facebook and Authorities:

   - Take proactive steps to report fraudulent activity encountered on Facebook to the platform's dedicated reporting channels. Use the built-in reporting features to flag suspicious accounts, posts, or messages for review by Facebook's security team.

   - Additionally, consider reporting scams to relevant authorities, such as consumer protection agencies, law enforcement agencies, or cybercrime reporting platforms. Provide as much detail and evidence as possible to aid in the investigation and prosecution of fraudulent actors.

4. Participating in Online Safety Workshops and Training:

   - Take advantage of online safety workshops, webinars, or training programs offered by reputable organizations or cybersecurity experts. These resources provide valuable insights into best practices for protecting yourself and others from online scams and threats.

   - Stay engaged with online safety communities and forums where users share experiences, advice, and resources related to cybersecurity and scam prevention. Collaborate with fellow members to exchange insights and support each other in staying safe online.

5. Continuously Updating Security Measures:

   - Regularly review and update your security measures and privacy settings on Facebook to mitigate potential risks and vulnerabilities. Enable two-factor authentication, use strong, unique passwords, and employ privacy controls to limit who can access your profile and information.

   - Stay informed about Facebook's latest security features and updates, and take advantage of any new tools or safeguards introduced by the platform to enhance your protection against scams and fraudulent activities.

By prioritizing ongoing education and awareness, you empower yourself and others to navigate the digital landscape of Facebook with confidence and resilience. Remember that collective vigilance and proactive engagement are instrumental in creating a safer and more secure online environment for everyone. Together, we can work towards building a community where scams and fraudulent activities have no place to thrive.

Conclusion:

In the intricate web of social media interactions, Facebook serves as both a virtual marketplace and a platform for connectivity. However, amidst the endless scroll of posts and profiles lies the lurking threat of scams and fraudulent activities. Yet, fear not, for armed with the knowledge gleaned from this guide, you possess a powerful shield against such digital perils.

As we conclude this journey through Safebook, let us reflect on the invaluable lessons learned. We have delved into the depths of scam tactics, from the deceptive allure of phishing links to the enticing promises of bogus investment opportunities. We have scrutinized profiles and pages, honing our ability to discern authenticity from deceit. We have exercised caution in our communication, guarding against the siren call of suspicious messages and friend requests. And we have embraced the role of educators, disseminating our wisdom to friends and family, creating a ripple effect of awareness throughout our digital communities.

But our journey does not end here; it is merely the beginning of a vigilant and empowered approach to navigating the digital landscape. As we step forward, let us remain vigilant, ever watchful for the signs of potential scams and fraudulent activities. Let us continue to safeguard our personal information, to verify authenticity, to exercise caution in our interactions, and to educate ourselves and others.

For in doing so, we not only protect ourselves but also contribute to the collective resilience of our digital community. Together, let us forge a safer, more secure online environment—one where trust and authenticity prevail, and scams find no fertile ground to take root.

As you embark on your continued journey through the digital realm, remember the lessons of Safebook: knowledge is your armor, vigilance your shield, and community your strength. With these tools at your disposal, may you navigate the vast expanse of Facebook with confidence, resilience, and peace of mind. Stay safe, stay vigilant, and may your digital adventures be filled with authenticity, connection, and joy.

www.ingramcontent.com/pod-product-compliance
Lightning Source LLC
Chambersburg PA
CBHW070734260726
48660CB00007B/2834